TOURETTE SYNDROME

TOURETTE SYNDROME

Ruth Bjorklund

Marshall Cavendish
Benchmark
New York

Many thanks to Deb, Jenny, Julia, Elizabeth, and Bernadette

Marshall Cavendish Benchmark
99 White Plains Road
Tarrytown, New York 10591-5502
www.marshallcavendish.us

Library of Congress Cataloging-in-Publication Data

Bjorklund, Ruth.
Tourette syndrome / by Ruth Bjorklund.
p. cm. — (Health alert)
Summary: "Provides comprehensive information on the causes, treatment, and history of tourette syndrome"—Provided by publisher.
ISBN 978-0-7614-3985-1
1. Tourette syndrome—Juvenile literature. I. Title.
RC375.B56 2010
616.8'3—dc22
                    2008051243

Front Cover: A strand of DNA
Title page: People with Tourette syndrome can sometimes say things involuntarily, although this happens rarely

Photo research by Candlepants Incorporated

Cover Photo: Thomas Northcut / Getty Images

The photographs in this book are used by permission and through the courtesy of:
Getty Images: Thatcher Keats, 3; David Job, 5, 40; Richard Freeda, 7; Michael Malyszko, 9; Thomas Northcut, 13,; Zigy Kaluzny, 15; Dr. Dennis Kunkel, 16; 3D4Medical.com, 17; 19, 43, 50, 37; Anna Huerta, 23; Laurence Monneret, 35; Michael Rosenfeld, 38; Bob Thomas, 47; Tim Macpherson, 49; Alex Mares-Manton, 52. *Photo Researchers Inc.*: Paul Brown, 21; Scimat, 44. *Art Resource, NY*: Erich Lessing , 27, 30. *The Image Works*: Mary Evans Picture Library/Sigmund Freud Copyrights, 29; World History / Topham, 33. *Alamy Images*: Food Drink and Diet/MarkSykes, 41.

Editor: Joy Bean
Publisher: Michelle Bisson
Art Director: Anahid Hamparian

Printed in Malaysia
6 5 4 3 2 1

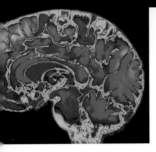

CONTENTS

1

WHAT IS IT LIKE TO HAVE TOURETTE SYNDROME?

Jo was not a happy baby or toddler. She was overly active, easily frustrated, and frequently angry with her parents and her day care teachers. By the time she was five, she had two new brothers. She was not very fond of them, either. She often stormed through the house hitting things and hollering. When Jo's tantrums got out of control, her mother would send her to a "quiet room." Jo's bedroom was painted her favorite color, yellow, and there were stuffed animals and colorful posters on the walls. But the family doctor said that Jo needed a quiet, calm space to relax in. "We painted a room in the house light blue, and added soft lighting and lots of pillows and blankets. There was nothing to throw or hit or damage. It was a **stimulant**-free place," Jo's mother says. "I wanted her to be safe."

When Jo started school, her behavior did not change. She did not cooperate with her teacher, and she was not making new friends. Her worried mother spoke to Jo's **pediatrician**. He said Jo was a very high-strung child. He suspected that she had **attention deficit hyperactivity disorder (ADHD)**. ADHD is a commonly diagnosed disorder of children in the United States. People who have ADHD have difficulty paying attention, sitting still, taking turns, and being patient.

Unexplainable anger in young children can sometimes be a symptom of Tourette syndrome.

Jo's mother believed that while some of ADHD's symptoms applied to her child, they did not explain all of Jo's behaviors. School and home life continued to grow more challenging for Jo. She often came home angry with her teachers and classmates. At home, she fought constantly with her brothers.

On another visit to the doctor, Jo's mother described Jo's anger and inability to get along with others. The doctor said that medications might help. Jo's mother did not want to give her young daughter medicine, yet she was terribly worried about Jo's future.

Jo started treatment for ADHD. Medicines that help people with ADHD are stimulants. They reduce hyperactivity and improve a person's ability to focus and cooperate. A stimulant is a chemical that generally increases energy, like the caffeine in coffee. But in people who have ADHD, stimulants do the opposite—they calm people down.

The ADHD medicine calmed some of Jo's behaviors. But it also made her sleepy during the day. "Jo and her brothers and I used to ride our bicycles down to the beach all the time. But once she started taking so many naps, we could not go anymore," Jo's mother recalls sadly.

Not long after Jo started taking the medicine, her behavior started to change. She frequently made growling noises and shrugged her shoulders for no clear reason. She had long bouts of coughing without being sick. She started repeating words.

"Sometimes when I drove her to school, she would say 'mom' what seemed like forty-five times in a row," says Jo's mother.

Finally, Jo went to see a **pediatric neurologist**, a children's doctor who specializes in disorders of the brain. The neurologist saw that Jo made sounds and movements that she could not control. "We cannot really test for it, but I think Jo has Tourette syndrome," the doctor said. She went on to say that a lot of children with Tourette syndrome appear to have ADHD when they are young. But when doctors prescribe stimulants to treat ADHD, the stimulants often trigger **tics**. That is when doctors realize that their patients likely have more than ADHD and that

The first step in determining if someone may have Tourette syndrome is for him or her to get an examination by a doctor.

they most likely have Tourette syndrome instead of (or in addition to) ADHD.

Jo's neurologist explained that Tourette syndrome is a disorder that affects the chemicals in the brain. The chemicals were causing Jo to make **involuntary** movements and to utter involuntary sounds. These actions are called tics.

Jo stopped taking the ADHD medicine, but her tics did not stop. They became stronger and happened in bouts—her eyes would blink, and her shoulders would shudder and twitch. She would say words over and over.

Her tics made it very hard for Jo to do schoolwork. "If she were doing math homework, for example, and her tics interrupted her, she would have to start her math all over again," her mother explains.

When she had terrible tics in her shoulders, Jo would sometimes lie on the floor to try and keep her body relaxed. Stress always made the tics worse. "It was so hard to watch, and it looked so painful," Jo's mother says. Jo said that it did not hurt as much as it might look. But after a day with a lot of tics, her muscles did ache.

Although the family was relieved to know what Jo's health problems really were, they did not know how to help her. There are medicines that can help control tics, but they have **side effects.** Jo and her parents decided to try a new medicine called **clonidine.** This medicine lowers blood pressure and is also useful in helping people quit smoking. The clonidine helped calm Jo's tics, but it made her very sleepy. "I think she slept through most of third grade," says her mother. The medicine also caused Jo to gain weight. But she did feel better. "We have a family joke," says Jo. "Whenever anyone asks how I am doing I say, 'Good, and tired!'"

Whenever Jo or her family would tell anyone about Jo's syndrome, people would always ask, "Is that the disease where people swear all the time?" It is true that in very rare and very severe cases of Tourette syndrome, people curse when they have vocal tics, but hardly anyone has that symptom. "It is the Hollywood version [of Tourette syndrome]," says Jo.

Instead of giving Jo pills every day, Jo's doctor prescribed her medicine to be taken as a skin patch. Jo wears the patch for three days before changing it. The dose is smaller and is released into her body on a regular basis, so she does not become as tired. Jo exercises more, and that also helps to control her tics. She has fewer tics now and is doing much better in school. Jo has also made some new friends. "I have a job walking my neighbor's dog every day after school," Jo says proudly. "And I have lots more energy and I feel much better than I used to." "We *all* do," Jo's mother says with a smile.

2

WHAT IS TOURETTE SYNDROME?

Tourette syndrome (sometimes called Tourette disorder) is named after Georges Gilles de la Tourette, a nineteenth-century French physician. It is a relatively common disorder—up to 10 out of 1,000 Americans have more than one symptom, and millions more people worldwide have the disorder. Usually Tourette syndrome is discovered in children between the ages of five and eight, when tics generally first appear. More boys than girls develop the disorder. Scientists believe Tourette syndrome may be caused by a combination of **genetic** (inherited from parents) and environmental sources. Symptoms include sudden, involuntary muscle movements called tics, including vocal tics. Symptoms range from mild to severe. Tourette syndrome can be a lifelong condition, but symptoms sometimes lessen as a young person becomes an adult.

Tourette syndrome is a disorder, not a disease. There are no tests for the condition. A person is diagnosed when he or she has a frequent pattern of physical or vocal tics. A specialist on Tourette syndrome, Dr. Roger Freeman, defines it as "simply a multiple, changing pattern of tics, including at least one noise-making tic." He says that the tics do not have to happen at the same time, but they must occur for at least twelve months in a row. Freeman diagnoses Tourette syndrome no matter how strong or mild his patients' symptoms are.

Scientists do not know for sure what causes Tourette syndrome. However, it is clear that the disorder can run in families. Doctors once thought Tourette syndrome was so unlikely that they rarely diagnosed it. Today, doctors are aware that Tourette syndrome is more common than they once thought, so they are able to make more accurate diagnoses. As a result, many people diagnosed today have no idea if someone in their family had the disorder.

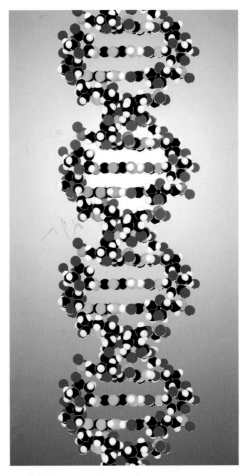

Each DNA strand contains gene molecules that are passed on from your parents.

Pinpointing a Diagnosis

Doctors do not recognize Tourette syndrome much before age five or six, when physical tics begin. If the tics are very mild, such as eye blinking, parents and doctors may not think anything is wrong with the child. On the other hand, symptoms are often mistaken for other disorders. One parent agrees, saying, "If a child scrunches his eyes, he is sent off to an eye doctor; and if a child hunches her shoulders, she had better get her back checked out." The difficulty in detecting the disorder is that people with Tourette syndrome experience tics only at certain times, so they do not necessarily have them during a visit to the doctor. The tics also change. Physical tics tend to increase with age. Vocal tics come later. There are no tests that identify Tourette syndrome and there is no way to measure it. Doctors must rely on observation, a patient's genetic background, and a patient's history of behaviors.

If a patient has **Tourette syndrome plus**, the diagnosis is even more difficult to make. Symptoms of ADHD or **obsessive-compulsive disorder (OCD)** appear at an earlier age and are usually very noticeable, especially once a child starts attending school and his or her behavior can be compared to other students' behavior. Doctors often prescribe medications to ease the symptoms of these **comorbid** disorders, but the medications can intensify the tics. The increase in tics may help the doctor diagnose Tourette syndrome, but it also makes treatment more complicated. Drugs that help one disorder may cause the other disorder to get worse. A filmmaker who made a movie about Tourette syndrome says, "People do not know. It is tough to get a diagnosis. You go through eight or ten doctors even now. It is a hard thing."

A teacher may notice a difference in the behavior of a child who has Tourette syndrome compared to a child who does not.

Most researchers say that an abnormal **gene** (or genes) is the likely cause of Tourette syndrome. A gene is a small biological unit in living organisms. It transfers characteristics, such as eye color, from parents to children. Many genetic diseases and physical traits require that the gene come from both parents. However, scientists think Tourette syndrome is **autosomal**—that is, only one gene from either parent can cause the symptoms.

The faulty gene or genes in Tourette syndrome affects two areas of the brain—the **cerebral cortex** and the **basal ganglia**. The cerebral cortex is a thin layer of gray matter that covers the brain. It is made up of nerve cells, called **neurons**, and the pathways that connect them. This region is responsible for

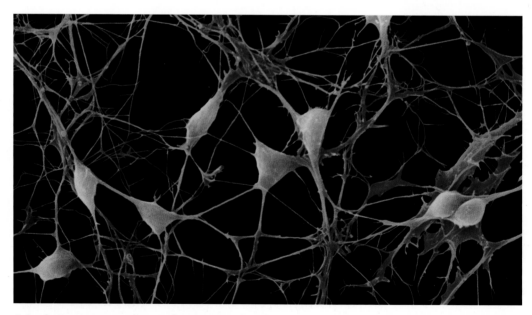

A look at neurons under a microscope.

thinking, memory, language, problem solving, social skills, and fine motor function. Fine motor skills involve controlled movement in the hands, fingers, wrists, toes, feet, lips, and tongue. The basal ganglia (plural for ganglion) are groups of neurons that control coordination and movement. Neurons are separated by tiny gaps called **synapses.** Electric impulses carrying information from one neuron to the next must leap across the synapses, and they are aided by chemicals called **neurotransmitters.** Researchers think that the abnormal gene or genes in Tourette syndrome affects the levels of some of the neurotransmitters in the brain. The three most important neurotransmitters involved are **norepinephrine**, **dopamine**, and **serotonin.**

An illustration of a synapse between neurons.

Oliver Sachs, "An Anthropologist on Mars"

Oliver Sachs is a famous neurologist who has written numerous books and articles about disorders of the brain. He was born in London. His mother was a surgeon, and his father was a family doctor. His parents often told him about their medical experiences, so Oliver discovered at a young age that practicing medicine was more about people and their stories than simply about science. He became fascinated with the brain and its many mysteries. Once he became a doctor, he began writing about his patients' extraordinary lives. One of his books, *Awakenings*, became a movie. Another book, *The Man Who Mistook His Wife for a Hat*, became a play.

Sachs has raised awareness about many overlooked disorders, such as autism, epilepsy, Parkinson's disease, schizophrenia, and Alzheimer's disease. He writes about many other neurological conditions as well, but he calls Tourette syndrome his "favorite."

Dr. Sachs admires people who struggle with Tourette syndrome and believes that they show extraordinary and creative strength in dealing with the disorder. One of the stories in his book, "An Anthropologist from Mars," is about a Canadian surgeon who has wild, lunging tics that completely disappear when he operates. Dr. Sachs feels that it is very important to tell his patients' stories so that others can learn more about what Tourette syndrome feels like "from the inside." Many people with Tourette syndrome appreciate his interest, his research, and his support.

Some scientists believe that Tourette syndrome might not always be genetic. Instead, an abnormal gene might develop while the fetus is growing, or a brain injury or trauma might change the neurotransmitters. Whether Tourette syndrome is genetic or not, scientists agree that environmental factors such as allergies, medicines, foods, fatigue, or emotional and physical stress can make symptoms worse.

SYMPTOMS

The chief symptoms of Tourette syndrome are tics. Physical tics are brief, irregular, involuntary movements, and vocal tics are sounds or words that are repeated for no apparent reason. Tics are usually unpredictable, although certain triggers, such as being sick or anxious, can aggravate them. Most people describe a tic as a powerful urge. Though tics can happen against people's will, sometimes individuals can stifle tics for a short period of time. But as people try to rein in their tics, the urge becomes more intense, which creates discomfort and stress. After holding back for a while, many people burst out in a flurry of tics.

The strength of Tourette symptoms varies widely. The tics may be so mild that they are unnoticeable. Or they may be serious enough to interfere with daily living. Most tics are rapid, while others cause people to freeze in position suddenly. Mild physical tics include eye blinking, shoulder shrugging,

Artwork representing a person suffering from Tourette syndrome speaking out with involuntary noises. Saying inappropriate words out of context, called coprolalia, is an extremely rare (though frequently publicized) vocal tic that affects less then 10 percent of persons with Tourette syndrome.

head twitching, and sticking out the tongue. Mild vocal tics include sniffing, sneezing, spitting, coughing, grunting, and throat clearing.

A Free and Equal Education

There are two important federal laws that give students with Tourette syndrome and other disabling conditions extra help in school if they need it. One is a civil rights law called Section 504 of the Rehabilitation Act of 1973, which provides special help through a program called a 504 Plan. The other is an education law called the Individuals with Disabilities Education Act (IDEA). It allows students with disabilities to receive help from an individual education plan (or IEP). At least once a year, students, teachers, therapists, and parents have a meeting to set out goals for the student as well as methods to help the student succeed.

Students with Tourette syndrome who are able to attend regular education classes will likely have a 504 Plan. Students who have Tourette syndrome-plus or other health issues usually have an IEP, which provides for more specialized education assistance.

Included in either a 504 Plan or an IEP are the following:

- pencil grips or use of a computer for students whose hands shake because of tics or medicines
- use of special places to study or to calm down, such as a resource room, library, or nurse's office
- a special pass so that students can quietly signal teachers that they need to leave the room
- flexible testing, such as taking untimed or extended-time tests, or oral tests for those who have difficulty keeping their hands steady
- being excused from completing some assignments
- a personal education aide (sometimes called a paraprofessional or "parapro") who can help with behavior control or schoolwork

A quiet space to relax is guaranteed to students under the 504 Plan.

Severe Tourette syndrome (sometimes called full-blown Tourette syndrome) is quite rare. Severe motor tics use many muscle groups and cause complex movements such as jumping, kicking, hopping, and spinning. They may also include more disturbing behaviors such as hitting, biting, imitating other people's actions, obscene gestures, or acts of self-injury such as picking scabs, rubbing wounds until they are raw, or biting or hitting one's self. Severe vocal tics include animal sounds; speaking words out of context, such as singing advertising jingles or saying a phrase over and over; repeating one's words, such as "I am tired, tired, tired," repeating the last sound someone else has made; or cursing. Cursing due to Tourette syndrome is very rare.

DIAGNOSING TOURETTE SYNDROME AND OTHER DISORDERS

There are other disorders that resemble Tourette syndrome. Many of these disorders are a lot more common, so doctors tend to diagnose them first before they realize that their patient has Tourette syndrome. Sometimes patients have more than one disorder. Some scientists believe that the multiple disorders may come from a common cause, such as a brain injury, a faulty gene, or a problem with chemicals in the brain. When there are two or more disorders along with Tourette syndrome, doctors called it a comorbid condition, or Tourette syndrome plus. Some comorbid disorders are attention deficit hyperactivity disorder (ADHD), obsessive-compulsive disorder (OCD), **Asperger syndrome**, and **oppositional-defiant disorder (ODD).** A person with Tourette syndrome may also have learning disabilities or sensory problems.

3

THE HISTORY OF TOURETTE SYNDROME

In the 1990s, several articles were published about whether or not the famous eighteenth-century musician Wolfgang Amadeus Mozart had Tourette syndrome. It will probably never be known for certain, but even if he did have the disorder, Mozart's doctors would have had no name for it, nor would they have any idea how to treat it. There were probably people who had Tourette syndrome in ancient times. But physicians and historians did not recognize the disorder. Instead, they thought their patients were possessed or enchanted by evil forces. A disease called Sydenham chorea (also called St. Vitus's dance), which had similar symptoms of physical and vocal tics, was thought to be the same disease as Tourette syndrome. But in 1686, British doctor Thomas Sydenham, after whom the disease was named, said that St. Vitus's dance was caused by a bacterial

Famous musician Wolfgang Amadeus Mozart may have suffered from Tourette syndrome.

infection. So people who had never had the infection—yet had vocal and physical tics—could not explain their condition. Not until 1825 did doctors begin recognizing and describing the symptoms of Tourette syndrome.

In the early part of the nineteenth century, a noblewoman named the Marquise de Dampierre had uncontrollable physical and vocal tics. Though she was raised with good manners and was otherwise very polite, the marquise shocked her well-mannered friends by suddenly cursing and shouting during ordinary social gatherings. Alarmed, her family sought the help of a French physician named Jean Itard, who was famous for educating a wild boy found living alone in a forest. Dr. Itard studied the actions of the marquise and believed that he could teach her to stop cursing by making her feel ashamed. The family never allowed the marquise to become Dr. Itard's patient, but the doctor left behind many important research notes that inspired later physicians.

Once Dr. Itard put the marquise's symptoms in writing, other scientists recognized other people with similar problems. According to some early theories, the condition was psychological. Others claimed it was physical. A French psychiatrist, Ernest Billod, thought that everyone had dark, evil thoughts and that only a person's willpower prevented him or her from acting and speaking outrageously. He said that people have "the power of not expressing all the ideas that come to our mind . . ." but that the marquise's "will submits to other forces." Another French doctor, David Didier Roth, published a book describing the case histories of six other people with similar symptoms. He concluded that they had muscle problems in their throats.

In the 1880s, a well-known neurologist named Jean-Martin Charcot was very interested in the marquise's condition. In his lectures he described the marquise as "someone of the most aristocratic part of society, who was known for uttering filthy words." In 1885, a student of Dr. Charcot, Georges Gilles de la Tourette, described the

Jean-Martin Charcot.

condition and called it a *maladie de tics* (French for "tic sickness"). Dr. Charcot, impressed by his student's work, named the disorder after Tourette.

Though Tourette is well-known for studying the disorder, many of his theories have been proven wrong. For example, he believed that the condition was a sickness in men but that it was just hysteria in women. He also believed that the syndrome

A lesson on hysteria is given at a hospital in the nineteenth century.

began with small tics and steadily increased into loud cursing and yelling. Dr. Tourette noted that the syndrome seemed to run in families. In the United States, a neurologist named George Beard described jumping behaviors and muscle tics in a group of French-Canadian lumberjacks in Maine. The lumberjacks would leap or jump or throw knives while repeating words constantly. Dr. Beard also believed the condition was hereditary.

Dr. Tourette believed the maladie de tics was a disease that grew steadily worse. But doctors treating patients with similar symptoms did not think their patients had the same disease because their symptoms did not worsen. One, Dr. Guinon, said that when his patient was not suffering from a bout of tics, she was completely normal. He wrote that she had "not the tiniest grimace, not the smallest convulsive tic of the limbs." Her illness did not become more severe as she aged.

In the early part of the twentieth century, doctors remained divided about the cause and treatment of Tourette syndrome. Two doctors, Henry Meige and E. Feindel, published a book called *Tics and Their Treatment*. In the book, they state that tics are a "nervous weakness." Jean-René Cruchet, a French doctor, disagreed with this idea. He felt that his patients could not help themselves from having tics. In the 1920s, some physicians suspected that the disorder was brought on by infections or lesions on the brain. At the same time, other doctors believed Tourette syndrome was a psychological problem. The famous psychoanalyst Sigmund Freud had a patient with physical and vocal tics. Dr. Freud decided that his patient suffered from "hysterical trauma." Until the middle of the twentieth century, most doctors accepted Freud's view of Tourette syndrome and treated it as a psychological problem.

As doctors continued to disagree, one thing was obvious— Tourette syndrome was a very complicated condition. In 1965, an American husband-and-wife medical team, Arthur and Elaine Shapiro, successfully treated a Tourette patient with medicine. They published their research in the *British Journal of Psychiatry*. In the article, the Shapiros wrote that the medicine's success proved that Tourette syndrome is a neurological disorder and not a psychological problem. At first, most other doctors took little notice because they thought the disease was very rare. But a reporter from *Today's Health* magazine wrote an article about the Shapiros' research, and immediately the magazine's office was flooded with mail from excited patients and parents of children with similar symptoms. It soon became clear to doctors that there were many more patients with Tourette syndrome than they had ever realized.

In 1972, Dr. Arthur Shapiro joined patients and their parents to establish the Tourette Syndrome Association. He also published a book called *Gilles de la Tourette Syndrome*. Because of the Shapiros' research, doctors and patients have a greater understanding of the disorder.

Sigmund Freud believed Tourette syndrome was a psychological disorder.

Learning About Tourette Syndrome

The Tourette Syndrome Association is a national organization, but there are regional and local chapters that can put people in touch with community resources. One regional member is Bernadette Witty, a mother of three who has Tourette syndrome. She often makes school visits to talk about the disorder. "It's not a simple disorder," she says. "In school, everyone wants to fit the mold, pay attention, and get everything done. That is so hard to do, and many people say, 'Give me the name of the pill, so I can make it go away.'" A pill won't make it go away, says Ms. Witty. But education can help students and teachers take some of the mystery out of Tourette syndrome. Ms. Witty and members of the Tourette Syndrome Association have books, videos, and packets of information they can share with teachers, classmates, family doctors, and others. They also can make school visits or be a part of teacher training programs. "I remember having tics during my exams at school and the teacher thought I was cheating because I kept looking to my left!" Ms. Witty tells students when she visits classrooms. "It is hard enough to pay attention and do the best you can on a test and have to try and handle your tics as well. You spend as much time concentrating on not having tics as you do trying to do your schoolwork." Ms. Witty reminds students that a person with Tourette syndrome cannot control the tics any more than a person using a wheelchair can jump up and walk away. After her school visits, classmates and teachers have a better understanding of the challenges a person with Tourette syndrome faces. They also recognize and accept that people with Tourette syndrome have talents and dreams just like theirs.

MODERN ADVANCES

Researchers today agree that the study and treatment of Tourette syndrome continues to pose as many questions as answers. Tourette syndrome has several conditions that are closely related, and each often needs its own form of treatment. Thus, a person with Tourette syndrome may be treated with a combination of medication, psychiatric and behavioral therapy, antibiotics, training in social skills and stress reduction methods, and a special diet.

Receiving a head massage is an alternative stress reduction method that may help Tourette syndrome sufferers.

Famous People with Tourette Syndrome

....

Long before Tourette syndrome was a recognized disorder, there were likely many famous people who never knew the name of their condition. Since Tourette syndrome was defined, we know about many famous people who live (or lived) with the disorder:

Dan Ackroyd—comedian and actor
David Beckham—soccer player
Dr. Samuel Johnson—British poet and essayist
Howard Hughes—aviator
Howie Mandel—comedian and actor
Jim Eisenreich—baseball player
Michael Wolff—jazz musician
Tim Howard—soccer player and Olympic athlete

David Beckham.

A young man gets an EEG, which records electrical activity of the brain.

Because of the variety of symptoms, today's Tourette syndrome research involves a variety of approaches. Some scientists are studying how Tourette syndrome, or Tourette-like symptoms, can come from bacterial infections or brain injury. Traumas such as these may cause certain genes to mutate, or change. Other new technologies are helping scientists learn more about inherited abnormal genes so that they can improve genetic counseling to future parents and help doctors diagnose the disorder sooner.

Neuroimaging is a group of technologies used to take pictures of the brain. Neuroimaging devices include **EEGs (electroencephalograms)**, **PET (positron emission tomography) scans**, **CT (computed tomography) scans**, and **MRI (magnetic resonance imaging)**. Each has helped researchers see inside the brain. CT scans and MRIs map portions of the brain involved with physical and vocal tics and reveal any scars, lesions, or injuries. A PET scan provides information about chemical changes in the brain, and EEGs give information about the nerve circuits in the brain.

Many of the symptoms of Tourette syndrome are treated with medications. Studies have shown that certain genes produce proteins that cause the level of some neurotransmitters to become too high or too low. The imbalance of neurotransmitters prevents the neurons from communicating with one another normally. In cases where tics interfere with a patient's quality of life, medications can often correct the levels of the neurotransmitters in the brain. Doctors prescribe time-tested drugs such as **haloperidol** and **pimozide**, as well as a class of drugs called **SSRIs (Selective Serotonin-Reuptake Inhibitors)**. Researchers continue to experiment with new drugs that may perform better with fewer side effects. Some experiments have shown that people with Tourette syndrome may also benefit

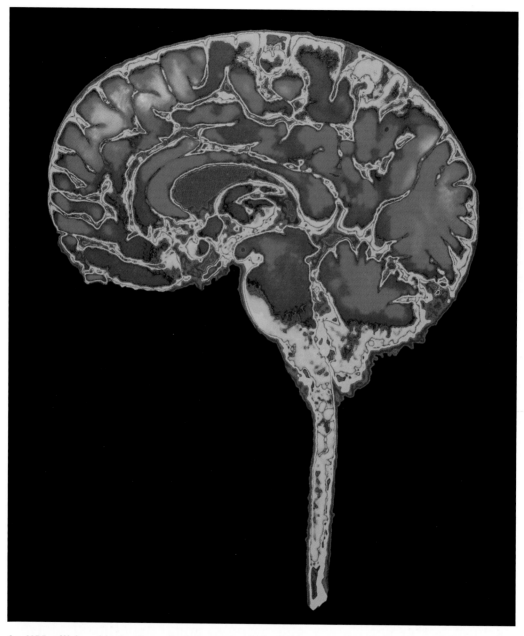

An MRI will be able to show doctors parts of the brain they would not be able to see otherwise.

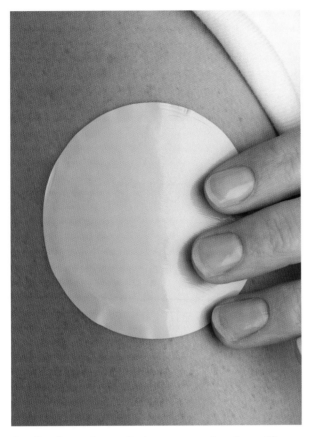

Studies have shown that some people who suffer from Tourette syndrome get relief from wearing a nicotine patch.

from injections of a neurotoxin produced by the bacteria *Clostridium botulinum* or even from wearing a nicotine patch. To test the effectiveness of newer treatments, many patients choose to help researchers and themselves by participating in clinical drug trials. Clinical drug trials are research experiments that test new drugs using patient volunteers.

Researchers continue to investigate causes and treatments of Tourette syndrome. It is an uncomfortable and sometimes extremely difficult disorder for people to live with. At this time, there is no cure or treatment that works for every patient, because every patient's experience is different. But overall, today's treatments offer a vast improvement in quality of life for people with Tourette syndrome.

4

COPING WITH TOURETTE SYNDROME

Each person with Tourette syndrome is affected in a different way. After a diagnosis, many people are frightened about what they may have to face in the future. But most people with Tourette syndrome have mild to moderate tics, and they can expect to live normal lives. People with stronger tics or additional health problems may have a more complex treatment plan that includes therapy and medication. However, Tourette syndrome is not fatal or contagious. There are many treatment options, and symptoms sometimes lessen as a person grows older.

PREVENTION

At this time, there is no way to prevent or predict whether a person will have Tourette syndrome. Genetic researchers are

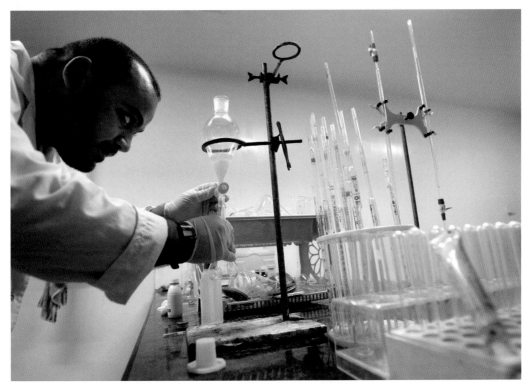

Scientists are always working toward finding a way to prevent Tourette syndrome.

trying to find the gene or genes that lead to developing the disorder. If they do, they will be closer to finding a way to prevent the disorder. There are many health organizations that support research in both the treatment and the cause of the disorder.

TREATING TOURETTE SYNDROME

The main goals of treating Tourette syndrome are to control physical and vocal tics and to help reduce symptoms of any related disorder, such as ADHD or OCD, or other involuntary impulsive actions. Treatment can include medications and therapies such as physical, occupational, psychological, and speech therapy.

Many people do not require medication. Their tics do not interfere enough with daily life to require medicine. Some people, however, have tics that prevent them from successfully studying in school or working at a job. For mild to moderate

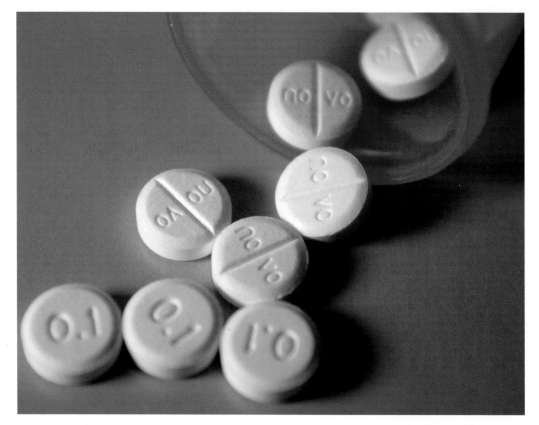

Clonidine is one medication that people who suffer from Tourette syndrome can take.

The Tic Code

. . . .

Jazz musician Michael Wolff is the inspiration behind the movie *The Tic Code*. Although having Tourette syndrome is not something he would wish for, Michael Wolff, a jazz piano player, says that when he plays his piano, his energy level soars and he rarely has tics. But, he says, "Sometimes you can control them; sometimes there is no way." Researchers and psychologists tend to agree that many people with Tourette syndrome see a slightly positive side to their disorder. By facing up to their challenges, many children with Tourette syndrome become exceptionally caring, focused, energetic, and fun loving.

tics, the most common drugs are ones developed for other health problems. Some blood pressure medicines seem to help control tics. Two other drugs that also help, clonidine and **guanfacine**, also help people quit smoking. Each of these drugs affects the chemistry of the brain. Some people experience side effects, such as sleepiness, dry mouth, or depression. Patients need to identify any side effects so that their doctors can prescribe different medicines or change dosage amounts.

FOCUS

Many people with Tourette syndrome say that when they are involved in their hobbies, they rarely have tics. By deeply focusing on something they really care about, they seem to prevent their symptoms. One writer in Los Angeles has Tourette syndrome, and so does his daughter. He says that when his daughter paints, her tics stop. He writes that both of them believe the disorder makes life more interesting.

For people with more severe tics, there are other types of drugs. **Neuroleptics** (sometimes called antipsychotics) and **atypical neuroleptics** act as tranquilizers that reduce the levels of the neurotransmitter dopamine in the areas of the brain that control movement and speech. **Aripiprazole**, a newer atypical neuroleptic, reduces dopamine, but it also raises dopamine in areas of the brain that have too little. For those with particularly strong tics, using the bacterium that causes botulism

People with Tourette syndrome sometimes find relief when they get involved in a hobby, such as painting.

has shown promise. Doctors inject the neurotoxin into the affected muscles, which relax for up to three months at a time.

People with Tourette syndrome plus have complicated treatment plans. Many of the medications used to treat ADHD or OCD often increase the severity and frequency of tics. Other side effects are restlessness, trouble sleeping, mental dullness, tremors, and weight gain.

Bullying

....

In just about any school, there are bullies. People who bully often have many problems of their own. They tease others in order to feel better themselves.

With their unusual vocal and physical tics, students with Tourette syndrome are often victims of school bullies. People who ridicule others rarely do so in public places such as the classroom or the cafeteria; instead they find secluded areas such as hallways, bathrooms, school buses, and playgrounds. A student can be bullied every day without a teacher or other adult ever seeing it happen.

Being bullied is a lonely and frightening experience. Many students feel that telling the teacher is tattling and will only encourage the teasing. But it is important to tell a parent or other trusted adult about the problem. Teachers and school administrators can help bring an end to the harassment. Bullies tend to single out people whom they fear or do not understand. Teachers can show their students how to accept one another's differences and how to develop empathy toward those with disabilities. Whether you are a victim, a friend, or just an onlooker, the right thing to do is to speak up.

Bullies may cause trouble for some children with Tourette syndrome because those with the disorder seem different from other people.

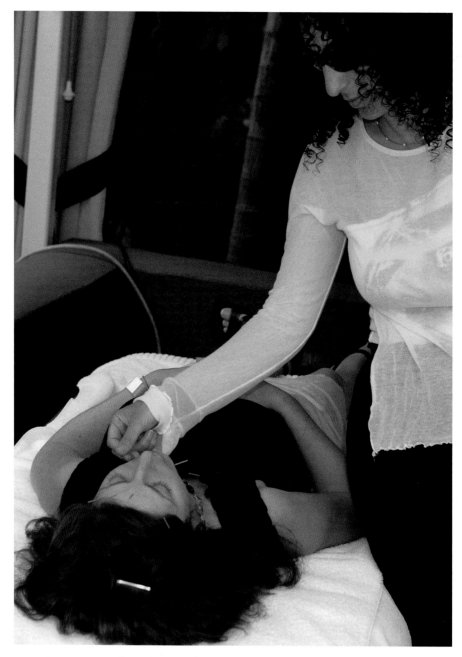

One alternative way of treating Tourette syndrome is with acupuncture.

OTHER TREATMENTS

Many people with Tourette syndrome benefit from other treatments besides medicine. Although Tourette syndrome is not a psychological problem, there are many psychological therapies that can help. Psychologists teach behavior skills, such as how to move on purpose whenever the urge to have a tic arises. Because stress can intensify tics, psychologists also teach techniques to reduce stress, such as breathing exercises and yoga. Other therapies include acupuncture and biofeedback. Acupuncture is an ancient Chinese therapy that uses thin needles inserted in special points of the body to open energy pathways. Biofeedback therapy uses a medical device with sensors that are attached to the body. The sensors detect tiny changes in muscle movement or tension and send feedback to patients that can help them control their involuntary actions.

TOURETTE SYNDROME AND SCHOOL

Although most students with Tourette syndrome have normal intelligence, many have some learning difficulties. In school, their tics can affect their ability to pay close attention or to read and write clearly. Students and their families often meet with teachers to discuss how to work with these problems. Some teachers allow students extra time on tests or a reduced amount of written homework. A student may ask for a classroom buddy—another student who can help with homework, note

Since may children with Tourette syndrome have trouble paying attention in class, they may need to get help by studying with a friend.

taking, or reading assignments. Teachers should also allow their students with Tourette syndrome freedom to leave the classroom and take a quiet break to calm their tics privately.

Some people with Tourette syndrome want to forego medicines in favor of managing their tics on their own. One school psychologist worked with a student who had Tourette syndrome from kindergarten through high school. When the student entered high school, he decided he would rather live with his tics than take medicine. After he stopped his medication, his tics increased and other students teased him more. But he had close friends, and he stayed positive about himself and the other students—even those who imitated him. He focused on his interests, such as karate and guitar, and his studies. Says the psychologist, "He is in college now, studying science. His tics are still pretty strong and he stutters, but he accepts that the symptoms of Tourette syndrome are part of who he is. He is the most kindhearted person I have ever known."

GLOSSARY

aripiprazole—A medication that lowers the neurotransmitter dopamine in some areas of the brain and raises it in other areas.

Asperger syndrome—A form of autism.

attention deficit hyperactivity disorder (ADHD)—A disorder that affects a person's ability to pay attention or to control his or her behavior.

atypical neuroleptics—Drugs that affect brain chemistry.

autosomal—Caused by receiving a specific gene from only one parent.

basal ganglia—Groups of nerve cells in the brain that control coordination and movement.

cerebral cortex—Gray matter covering the frontal area of the brain that controls thinking, memory, language, problem solving, social skills, and fine motor function.

clonidine—A blood pressure medication useful in controlling the tics of people with Tourette syndrome.

comorbid—Describing disorders that occur along with a primary disorder.

CT (computed tomography) scans—X-rays that take cross-sections of the body.

dopamine—A type of neurotransmitter.

EEGs (electroencephalograms)—Recordings of electrical activity in the brain.

gene—A basic biological unit that causes inherited traits such as eye color.

genetic—Caused by a person's genes.

guanfacine—A blood pressure medicine that is useful in treating tics.

haloperidol—An antipsychotic medication that is useful in controlling tics.

involuntary—Unable to be controlled.

MRI (magnetic resonance imaging)—A medical technique that uses magnetic fields to take pictures of the structure of the brain.

neuroimaging—Various procedures that take pictures of the brain.

neuroleptics—Drugs that affect brain chemistry.

neurons—A nerve cell.

neurotransmitters—A chemical that transmits signals between the nerve cells and the brain.

norepinephrine—A neurotransmitter.

obsessive-compulsive disorder (OCD)—A mental disorder in which a person is obsessed with certain thoughts, which lead him or her to perform specific acts repeatedly.

oppositional-defiant disorder (ODD)—A comorbid condition of Tourette syndrome that is expressed by extreme anger and an inability to obey rules.

pediatric neurologist—A children's doctor who specializes in treating disorders of the brain.

pediatrician—A children's doctor.

PET (positron emission tomography) scans—Medical procedures that detect chemical activity in the brain.

pimozide—A medication that helps control physical and verbal tics.

serotonin—A neurotransmitter found especially in the brain.

side effects—Adverse effects of a drug.

SSRIs (Selective Serotonin-Reuptake Inhibitors)—Drugs used to treat depression, anxiety disorders, personality disorders, and Tourette syndrome.

stimulant—Something that causes a person to become excited, alert, and wakeful.

synapses—The spaces between neurons.

tics—Involuntary physical or vocal activities.

Tourette syndrome plus—A diagnosis of Tourette syndrome that also includes other disorders.

FIND OUT MORE

Organizations

Jim Eisenreich Foundation for Children with Tourette Syndrome

Post Office Box 953

Blue Springs, MO 64013

1-800-442-8624

www.tourettes.org

National Center for Learning Disabilities

381 Park Avenue, Suite 1401

New York, NY 10016

1-888-575-7373

www.ncld.org

National Council on Disability

1331 F Street, Suite 850

Washington, DC 20004

1-202-272-2004

www.ncd.gov

Tourette Syndrome Association

42-40 Bell Boulevard

Bayside, NY 11361

718-224-2999

www.tsa-usa.org

Websites

Tourette Syndrome Online
www.tourette-syndrome.com

Tourette Syndrome Plus
www.tourettesyndrome.net

Growing up with Tourette's: Information for kids
http://tskids4.tripod.com/

Mayo Clinic
www.mayoclinic.org/tourette-syndrome/

Kids' Health
http://kidshealth.org/kid/health_problems/brain/k_tourette.html

Books and Films

Brill, Marlene Targ. *Tourette Syndrome*. Brookfield, CT: Twenty-First Century Books, 2002.

Buffolano, Sandra. *Coping with Tourette Syndrome: A Workbook for Kids with Tic Disorders*. Oakland, CA: New Harbinger Publications, 2008.

Halpern, Sue. *Introducing—Sasha Abramowitz*. New York: Farrar, Straus and Giroux, 2005.

I Have Tourette's but Tourette's Doesn't Have Me. HBO and the Tourette Syndrome Association. Home Box Office, 2005.

McCall, Steven Michael. *The Tyrannosaurus Tic: A Boy's Adventure with Tourette Syndrome*. Victoria, BC, Canada: Trafford Publishing, 2008.

INDEX

Page numbers for illustrations are in **boldface.**

Ruth Bjorklund lives on Bainbridge Island, near Seattle, Washington, with her husband, two children, and five pets. She has written several books about health issues for young people and is extremely proud of the members of her community who have Tourette syndrome and live interesting and courageous lives.